Easy Potty Training

How to Potty Train
Your Toddler

in 3 days

Merry Palmer

Table of Contents

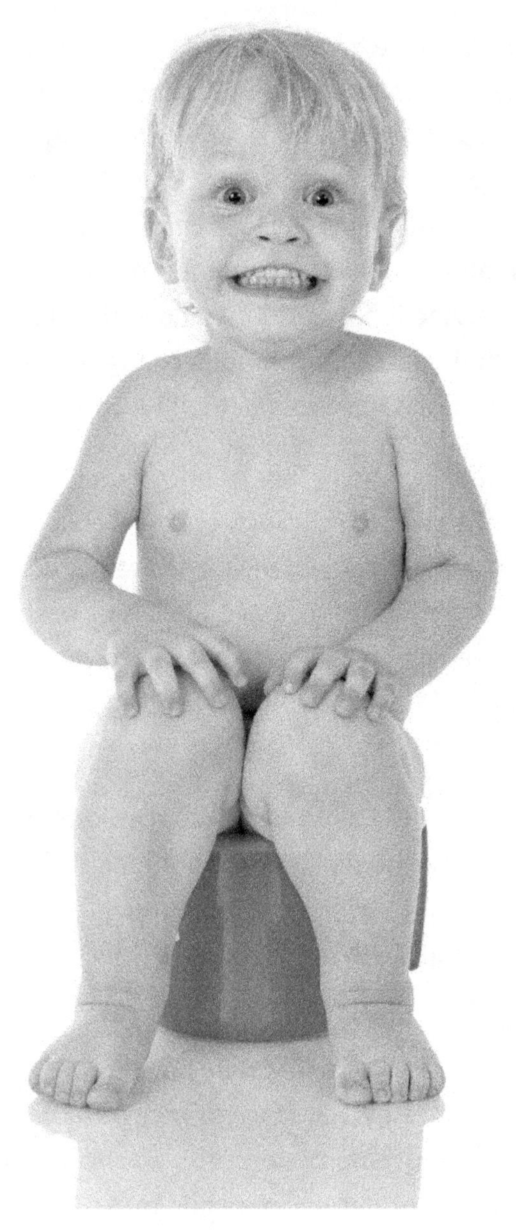

Introduction

From the moment you've had to change that first stinky diaper, you've probably been thinking about the fact that your child has to be potty trained at some point. Many parents are ecstatic to get the process going because they are tired of the diaper expense and the act of having to clean them, but what most parents don't realize is their children may *not* be ready for that moment to come. And it has nothing to do with your child being comfortable with the fact that someone changes their dirty diaper for them and they don't have to do anything about it.

Before we start looking at whether or not your child is ready for potty training, let's take a closer look at how a child's bladder and bowels develop. Believe it or not, children are not born with the capability of knowing when they have to go on a cognitive level, and if you try to begin potty training before they're able to recognize their body's signals, you're beating a dead horse, so to speak.

Before twelve months old, your baby has absolutely no control over their bowel movements. They cannot hold their bowels or bladder, and they will go whenever their body deems it necessary for them to void. That's why we invented diapers.

Between the ages of twelve months to eighteen months, your child will begin to recognize when they have to urinate. At around twenty-four months, they will start to recognize when they also must have a bowel movement; however, all children are different and develop at different paces. Your child might take until the age of three to recognize when they're going to have a bowel movement, and this is perfectly normal! There is nothing wrong with a child taking their time in the developmental stages.

In this book, we're going to explore how to figure out if your child is ready for potty training, preparing for potty training, how to potty train, how to handle regression, tips for boys and girls, common issues, nighttime potty training, and the main medical cause of potty training woes – constipation.

The final chapter is the easy working plan for potty training your toddler in 3 days!

Chapter One – When to Begin

As a parent of a child, you've been able to celebrate numerous milestones, such as their first smile, their first step, and their first word. However, one of the most milestones that parents look forward to most of any child's development is the day your child is potty trained. The average baby goes through almost 3,800 diapers before they're potty trained, and you've most likely changed your fair share, if not more, of those diapers.

Everyone loves their kids, but let's be honest, no one likes changing a dirty diaper. Becoming diaper free isn't just an exciting milestone for you, but it's an exciting time for your child. Your child will feel grown up when they're able to go to the bathroom on their own.

Unfortunately, there are numerous myths and bad methods out there for potty training kids. Let's look at the top four myths about potty training that could potentially sabotage your child's potty training efforts, as well as their development.

Myths

#1 Boys are more difficult to potty train than girls.

This is one of the most common and the oldest potty training myths out there. It doesn't matter if you're potty training a boy or a girl, the experience and the results ought to be the same. It's not any more difficult to potty train a boy than it is a girl, and many parents tend to overcomplicate things with boys.

However, boys ought to be potty trained the same way girls are.

#2 Making your toddler sit on the potty is going to train him or her.

There are many parents that believe putting their child on the potty teaches them how to use it on their own. However, this is a huge mistake. In fact, sitting on the toilet and trying will usually cause fear of the potty, which turns it into a fight.

#3 Daycare is going to potty train your child.

If you think the daycare center will potty train your child, you're sorely mistaken. The truth is daycares tend to turn away parents and their children who are not potty trained. The few daycares out there that still help with potty training do so in a way that's easiest for them. This method usually involves wearing pull-ups and trying every few hours on the toilet.

This is confusing for your child and makes the potty training process take much longer than necessary.

#4 Pull up style training pants are going to help.

Pull-up style training pants are just diapers with a different design and some clever marketing. They're diapers with a more expensive price tag, really.

Before disposable diapers were introduced in the Sixties, children were trained around eighteen months. This goes to show that children are capable of being trained at an earlier age; although, too early can be detrimental. You don't need pull-up style training pants in order to teach your child how to use the bathroom. In fact, many parents use the naked method, which means their child runs around without any diapers on at all, or pants!

Readiness

Parents all around you are boasting that their child was potty trained before they were two years old, but your child is over two and still not potty trained. So what is the right time to begin potty training? Kids are programmed with their own schedules for milestones when it comes to development, which is why it's important to allow them to set the pace for potty training.

So how do you know when they're ready to begin?

1. You're changing fewer diapers. Until around the age of twenty months, children urinate so often that expecting them to be able to control their bladder is a little unrealistic. However, toddlers who stay dry for an hour or two at a time are physically ready to begin potty training.
2. Your toddler's bowel movements are predictable, whether they happen after a meal, in the morning, or before bedtime; a regular rhythm is going to help you anticipate when you should take your child to the potty.
3. Your toddler is starting to show acknowledgement of their bodily functions. Some children will happily announce when a bowel movement is about to happen, and others will communicate through a less verbal manner. No matter what the signal is, if your child is aware of their bodily functions, then it's time to begin potty training.
4. Your toddler hates dirty diapers. At some point, many toddlers go through a small stage when they dislike personal messes. They're freaked out by sticky fingers and crumbs, and they're eager to get out of those soiled diapers as soon as they can. This is the best time to begin potty training because for the first time, your child hates those dirty diapers as much as you do.
5. Your child is able to perform simple undressing. When your toddler has to go, the potty isn't going to be of much use to

them if they can't quickly get their trousers down. In addition, girls should be able to hike their skirts quickly to get on the potty.

6. Your child understands bathroom vocabulary. Whether you like to use formal terminology or kid-friendly terms, if your child can understand them, then they're ready to begin potty training.

7. Your toddler wants to watch you go to the bathroom. If your toddler is demanding a live demonstration of going to the bathroom, then they want to do it, too.

Why Deadlines are Harmful

Many experts are beginning to argue that deadlines are harmful to children. After all, can you force a three-year-old who has Down syndrome to go to the bathroom? No, you can't, which is why the Attorney Generals' office of New Jersey has filed a discrimination suit against a preschool that expelled a toddler with this condition for failing to be potty trained.

Deadlines are convenient for the preschools, and they can even sound reasonable. However, they're based on the misunderstanding that toileting development of all children is the same, and there's the risk that the child could develop enuresis, which is daytime bedwetting and peeing accidents, or encopresis, which are defecating accidents.

When a toddler struggles with potty training, it means the child is not developmentally ready to begin or they're chronically constipated. Either way, potty training is doomed from the start, and the consequences can be long-lasting and severe.

Potty training deadlines can be the main reason why a child is having accidents. By setting a deadline for a three-year-old, a school is prompting parents to begin training at two or two and a half years old. The problem is most toddlers are not ready. They may be physically capable of using the toilet, but that's completely different from possessing the judgement to follow the body's instructions when nature calls.

Preschool potty training mandates run against a basic fact, that three-year-olds hate using the toilet. They like to play with toys and build their towers. At school, they might feel too embarrassed or excited to interrupt playtime in order to use the bathroom; therefore, they develop the habit of holding their urine and bowels.

Over time, the bowels will fill with feces, forming a hard, large lump that presses against the bladder. Holding pee will thicken and irritate that bladder wall. These stressed bladders will empty without warning, causing an accident. With some children, the stretched rectum will lose sensation, and feces will just fall out.

Research suggests that children who are potty trained before age two have triple the risk of later developing enuresis compared to children who are trained later. This doesn't mean training a twenty-six-month-old child is wise. It just means that training a twenty-three-month-old is an even riskier proposition.

Preschools are difficult to persuade when it comes to this because they don't see the consequences of their policies. Some children will develop problems at age three or four, and these kids are singled out and issued ultimatums later on. However, with many children, it will take until kindergarten or beyond for constipation to reach a critical point.

Many pediatrician's clinics are packed with kids who are tweens and teens that still have accidents, and these kids were trained early to meet their preschool's deadlines. Clinical research suggests that children are ready to be potty trained around age three, but this isn't a hard rule. In general, children should be trained when they show readiness, not in response to a date on a calendar.

In addition to ditching these deadlines, or at least easing up on the enforcement, preschools can make a positive impact on children by teaching them healthy habits. Parents should teach their children the following things as they're potty training.

1. Identify healthy bowel movements. Children should be pooping piles of mush, like soft, thin snakes or soft-serve ice cream.
2. Discuss what happens when they keep their feces and urine inside. Preschoolers are able to understand the concept of being constipated, so teach them what it means.

3. Schedule their bathroom trips for around every two hours. Children need encouragement and opportunity at the same time.
4. Watch your child closely for signs of constipation. Bowel movement frequency is not a reliable measure of constipation. Severely constipated children will have bowel movements multiple times per day because they don't fully go to the bathroom. The top two signs of constipation in a child are extra-large bowel movements or bowel movements formed like logs or pellets. Other signs are urgent or frequent urination, an itchy behind, or belly pain.
5. Instruct your child to put their feet on a stool when they're using the bathroom. Defecating in the squatting position will straighten the rectum, which will allow their feces to fall out easily. Children are not able to relax their rectal muscles when their feet are dangling.
6. Explain that accidents are never their fault. Though many adults will insist otherwise, potty accidents are not a behavioral issue, a lack of cooperation, or laziness. They're not within your child's control, and they're a mortifying experience. Shaming children who have had an accident will only make them feel worse. What they need is compassion, understanding, and medical attention for any issues that might be at hand, such as chronic constipation or urinary tract infections.

So you know your child is or is not ready for potty training, but what do you need in order to begin? We'll take a look at that in the following chapter.

Chapter Two – Preparing for Potty Training

If your toddler is staying dry through their naps, are able to undress quickly in order to go, and are aware of and articulate their bodily functions, then your child is exhibiting the signs that they're ready to begin potty training. However, don't get rid of those diapers just yet. There's still plenty of work to be done.

First, you need to establish the right mindset for you and your child during this exciting phase. Then, you need to get to it and show them. Finally, find the right materials.

Play Up the Positives

Before your child goes diaper-free for the first time, highlight all the benefits of using the toilet to your child. You could tell them wearing underwear is fun, or that soon they will be able to flush just like you! However, don't call your child's old habits babyish or tell them about how bad wearing diapers is. This could provoke your child into resistance, which can be detrimental to future potty training efforts.

Establish Bathroom Vocabulary

Some experts recommend that you use formal vocabulary, such as urinate and defecate, rather than using slang so that children won't be embarrassed by babyish talk when they're older. However, what's more important is to be consistent with what you use. Never refer to your child's diaper contents as being disgusting or gross. Your child will be much more comfortable going to the bathroom if they view elimination as a natural process and not something disgusting.

Commend All Grown-Up Behavior

Let your toddler know you support all of his or her blossoming maturity by praising feats such as sharing toys and drinking from a cup without spilling it. Don't demand too much, though. If your child feels pressure to perform, he or she might begin pining for the simpler days of being younger and act in accordance.

Read About It

Find a child-oriented potty training book and read it together. Don't feel that you need to hammer home that lesson or even compare your child to the characters. Just hearing about other children who are using the potty will help your child feel more comfortable about making that leap.

Provide Easy Access

You want to get into the habit of dressing your child in the right potty training clothes, which are pants that pull up and down easily, or skirts that are easy to pull up and hold. Once they're dressed right, practice that pull-down maneuver! Ask your child to pull down their pants before a diaper change and then pull them back up after it's finished. You can even turn it into a fun game or contest by seeing who can pull down their pants faster. Remember, there's no time to spare when nature calls for your child to go potty, so the more practice the better.

Show, Don't Tell

You can do all the explaining to your child about how to squat, wipe, and flush, but it'll be a lot more effective and efficient to just bring your child into the bathroom and demonstrate for them. Not all parents will be comfortable parting with modesty for this, so don't feel bad if you skip this step if it's not within your comfort zone.

Close the Gap between Diapers and the Potty

If you can, change your toddler's diapers in the room where their potty is located. This will reinforce the connection between the two subtly. After your toddler has a bowel movement in the diaper, bring him or her into the room so they can watch you flush it down the toilet. If your toddler is afraid of the flushing noise, then just dump it in and flush it later when your toddler isn't in the room.

Let Them Be the Teacher

Purchase or borrow a doll that wets itself and encourage your child to help their doll learn to use the bathroom. This boosts your child's sense of mastery and provides them with a greater sense of control over the entire potty process.

Find the Right Potty

Look for models that are durable and are not going to tip over when your toddler jumps up to check what's inside. For an added bit of excitement, you can always shop together for the potty and then wrap it as a gift. Once it's home, let your child personalize the potty with stickers and write their name on it. If your child wants to, let them carry around the potty and sit on it while he or she is clothed. Then remind your toddler what the potty is for.

Opt for Potty Seats

Some children will balk at the idea of using the baby potty and demand they use the grown up's potty instead. In this case, purchase a potty seat, which will attach to the toilet. Look for stable fitting ones because shaky seats can scare children right back into their diapers for weeks. They should have built in footrests that offer something push against during their bowel movements. Skip plastic urine deflectors because they can scrape your toddler's bottom during a dismount.

If you notice your toddler is about to go to the bathroom, suggest to your toddler that they do it on the potty rather than in their diaper. If the answer is an obvious no, then leave it be. Pushing too quickly too soon can be detrimental to your toddler's bathroom development, and sometimes, they're just not ready. Let's look at more do's and don'ts in the following chapter.

Chapter Three – Do's and Don'ts of Potty Training

Half the battle has been won. You've put down the groundwork, and now it's time to put that new potty to use. Different strategies are going to work for different children, but these do's and don'ts will get the job done in general.

Do's

- If you really want to switch to pull-ups, there's nothing wrong with them. When your child is just starting to use the potty, most parents want to play it safe with disposable underpants. Your child can pull them down just like underpants, but if there's an accident, the pull-ups absorb like a diaper and they can be ripped off like a diaper rather than pulled over the feet. Once your child has enjoyed some successes on the potty, then try to switch to some washable training pants.

- Let your toddler go bare bottom. To boost their awareness of their body's signals, let them run around with their lower half completely unclothed. It's difficult to ignore urine when there isn't a diaper to catch it. Keep the potty close so your child can act on their body's signals quickly.

- Choose clothing that is easy on and easy off. When your toddler has to go, there isn't going to be a moment to lose. While they get a handle on undressing, avoid any buttons, snaps, zippers, or clasps. Elastic waists are probably the best way to go.

- Watch your toddler closely. At this point, you could be better at detecting their body's signals than they are. Look for the obvious signs, such as straining or fidgeting, and gently ask your toddler if you expect they have to go. Even if you're too late and your toddler has already gone through the motions, have them sit on the potty anyway to reinforce what needs to happen.

- Offer praise when your toddler reports bodily functions. Even delayed mentions are worthy of praise; after all, it takes practice for a toddler to recognize signs of an impending bladder and bowel movement and make it to the potty on time.

- Keep your toddler motivated. Remind them using the potty means they are growing up. When you first begin, small tangible incentives will help. For each success, put a sticker on a calendar or a penny in a piggy bank. While your toddler becomes more comfortable using the bathroom, it's better to phase out the reward and allow their inner motivation to take over.

- Teach your toddler to check for dryness. This allows them to have a sense of control. If they're dry, give them a pat on the back or a hug, but don't criticize if your toddler is wet.

Don'ts

- Don't expect too much out of your toddler too soon. Even the most enthusiastic of toddlers will take a few weeks to master their potty proficiency. They can take as many steps backward as they do forward. If your expectations are too high, you could diminish your toddler's self-confidence.
- Don't punish, scold, or shame your toddler. No parent likes mopping up pee on the floor, but try to stay level-headed. If you overreact, you could discourage your toddler's attempts in the future.
- Never deny your toddler drinks. Many parents believe they have to ration fluids in order to cut their toddler's chances of having an accident; however, this approach is not healthy and not fair. It's also not effective. In fact, the better tactic is to increase your child's fluids to give them more opportunities to succeed.
- Never nag or force your toddler to go to the bathroom. Try to keep it casual when you remind your toddler about using the bathroom. Nagging is only going to bring about resistance. In addition, don't force them to sit or stay on the potty, even if you know they're about to go.
- Do not begin a bathroom battle. Arguing over potty time is sure to prolong the struggle of potty training. If you meet with complete resistance, then throw in the toilet paper for a few weeks and let it rest. Be patient. As you wait for your toddler to come around to potty training again, don't bring up the subject or compare them to their peers who are already potty trained.
- Never lose hope. This process can seem pretty endless, but your toddler will eventually realize that it's better to use the potty than to wear those diapers. It takes time, and some take longer than others.

So you know the do's and the don'ts about potty training, but one question many parents have is how do they handle regression? We'll explore that in the following chapter.

Chapter Four – Handling Regression

Regression can be frustrating and even frightening for some parents, but it's not the end of the world. Regression happens more often than most parents will admit, but it's easily handled. In this chapter, we're going to take a look at how you can deal with regression in your toddler.

Make Sure It's Real Regression

Rest assured that many toddlers experience regression during potty training; it's normal. However, ask yourself whether your child was really potty trained to begin with. It's common for some setbacks to happen during the first few months or years after potty training. However, a truly potty trained toddler should want to use the potty.

Therefore, children who have several accidents each day and do not seem to care about them are not potty trained. Consider whether your child was ready for potty training to begin with. If your child was, begin looking for ways to get back to it. If not, talk to your pediatrician about when they think your child could be ready.

Don't Overreact

If your child experience an accident, it's important not to show disappointment. Doing this will make them feel more anxious, which can lead to even more issues in the future. Despite the frustration of having to go back into diapers due to accidents and regression, do everything you can to be positive. When you check to see if your child is dry, cheer and clap if they are. If your child is not, then remain nonjudgmental, tell them they had an accident, and take them to the potty.

Remember to never yell or scold during potty training. You want your child to feel empowered and not worry that they're going to be punished if there's an accident.

Find Root Causes and Resolve Them

You won't stop setbacks if you're not addressing what's causing them. Try identifying the reasons for regression because addressing them is going to help your child return to where they were. For example, many children begin having accidents during a time of transition that could cause stress, like starting a new school or welcoming a new sibling into the home.

Odds are, once you've settled down, your child is going to master potty training again. Even if your child makes it through the day without accidents, they could happen at night. Many children are not dry at night for years after they're dry during the day. Nighttime and naptime control are different from daytime control.

Medical complications can also cause potty regression, and constipation is the most common one. If a child has a hard time having a bowel movement, they might steer clear of the bathroom completely to avoid having to push and strain. Be sure your child is getting enough water and fiber. If they're afraid of sitting on the potty altogether, then play games or read books while they're sitting on the toilet to make it more fun.

Give a Gentle Reminder to Go

Accidents tend to happen because a toddler is having too much fun playing or doing something else and they don't want to stop to go to the bathroom. To resolve this issue, explain that it's normal to forget to use the potty sometimes and reassure your toddler they're still a big girl or boy. Then, take them to the potty every few hours at home and ask teachers to make sure your child goes to the potty frequently. Gentle, simple reassurance and reminders to use the potty get children back on track. Encourage your child to use the potty when they first wake up, before a meal, before bedtime, and right before you leave the house.

Use Rewards to a Degree

You can give your toddler some incentives to stay dry, especially if these rewards worked the first time you went through potty training. Make a sticker chart and give them a sticker every time they make it to the potty. After a few days in a row where they're successful, give them a treat like a trip to get a toy or some ice cream.

However, keep in mind that rewards don't work for all children, and in some cases, they can create just as much anxiety as punishments do. That's why the best rewards are usually just your words.

Chapter Five – Potty Training Tips for Boys

While potty training for boys and girls is virtually the same, there are a few things you might want to keep in mind for boys. In this chapter, we're going to explore those tips.

Have a Man Show Him How

Sometimes, it's just going to be easier for a boy's father or a father-figure to show him exactly what has to be done. Oftentimes, mothers are on potty duty, or in the case of single mothers, there isn't a male role model in the home all the time. On average, boys actually take a little longer to potty train because they don't have male role models showing them what to do.

As much as mothers try, they can't show peeing while standing very well. There is no harm in mothers allowing their sons to see their mothers use the bathroom because boys tend to mimic their mothers in everyday situations, but having a man show him the ropes a few times wouldn't hurt. If Dad isn't around to show him, then why not ask an older brother, uncle, or a grandfather to show him what to do?

Let Him Decide to Sit or Stand

Your son might be showing you signs that he's ready to start potty training, such as alerting you about full diapers. So should you teach him to sit or stand when he goes to the bathroom? The goal isn't how your toddler does it, but to actually get them to use the potty. If they want to stand or sit, it doesn't matter. Boys should begin using the potty however they feel most comfortable. If they start out sitting, they can always switch to standing when they're more adept.

Target Practice Makes Perfect

So your boy is able to stand and use the potty, but when he does, he doesn't aim very well and you're cleaning up a lot of messes. Turning this task into a game is a great way to amp up potty practice participation. This is the fun part. Tinkle target or bright round cereals, such as Froot Loops, is a great way to teach your toddler to aim while they're peeing standing.

Go Nude

The warmer months are a great way to try out some nude time. When toddlers are nude, they're more aware of when it's time for them to go. That's because they can't just go in the diaper and keep doing what they're doing. However, be sure to remind them to go to the bathroom every twenty minutes or so because you'll be cleaning up a lot of messes otherwise. If there is an accident, never yell or get upset because this can cause issues in the future.

Incentives

Gifts are a great way to get your little boy to go to the bathroom. Whatever motivates your toddler use the potty is a win-win situation. Candies, extra story time in the evening, cheap toys, coloring books, or even a potty dance are all ways to get your toddler to use the bathroom.

Pack the Potty

You're a busy parent and you're always going to the grocery store, running the pet to the vet, or going to the park in the afternoons with your son. However, there are going to be moments when your toddler has to go while you're out, so what do you do when there isn't a potty area in sight? Even though you have a toddler, don't rely on trees or corners. Your son has to have consistency, so when you're on the go, you should pack some familiar supplies, such as adapter seats for public restrooms or a spare potty your toddler can use in the car. Have a favorite book packed with you to make your toddler feel more at ease. If you give stickers as rewards at home, then keep some in your purse for incentive when you're not home.

Try Underwear

Potty training has officially begun, but you're not sure what that means for getting rid of the diapers and slipping on the big-boy underwear. Timing is everything. When a toddler is able to stay dry for three hours or more, then you can consider putting on underwear. It's part training and part reward. Let your toddler pick out their new underwear to wear during this time, and then increase the time they get to wear them with the more success they have.

However, do expect there to be accidents! Just clean them up and remind your toddler they should go in the potty.

Chapter Six – Potty Training Tips for Girls

You learned about potty training for boys in the previous chapter, but what about potty training differences for girls? There are a few differences that might seem obvious to women, but if you're a father potty training a daughter, it can seem a little daunting. So let's go over the basics in this chapter.

Make it Fun

Little girls enjoy shopping just as much as the next woman, so begin by letting her pick out the underwear she wants to buy – Disney characters are an excellent start. As a backup, let her pick out some potty training pants, too. These can be used for times when you don't have a toddler-friendly toilet around, but bear in mind that when your toddler is ready to use the potty regularly, then she should only wear the underwear.

Let your daughter select the potty seat from amongst different colors and themes. In addition, if you can find them, consider grabbing some toilet paper in her favorite color. The key is to make it seem like potty training is just another fun activity, not a chore.

Begin with the Right Position

Your daughter should have her feet flat on the floor on a step stool so her pelvis is horizontal. Children must have something to push against, whether they're boys or girls. By having their feet planted firmly on something, your toddler is going to feel more secure, and she'll have an easier time pushing when she goes to the bathroom. She'll also be less afraid she's going to fall into the potty.

This position helps your daughter have fewer accidents, too. When girls dangle over the potty, their backside is lower than their knees, and some urine can get into the posterior area of the vagina, and the little puddle of pee left there leaks into her underwear when she stands up. Have her sit as far forward or back as she wants, but keep in mind that sitting too far forward could lead to some unwanted leakage.

Teach the Proper Wiping Technique

While it's more sanitary for both girls and boys to wipe from front to back, it's imperative for girls to follow this technique for wiping. This helps them avoid introducing bacteria into their urinary tracts, which can lead to uncomfortable infections. Most girls who are below the age of five cannot wipe themselves properly. Help her wipe whenever she uses the potty.

It could be tempting to purchase disposable wipes, but you don't have to. Wipes have chemicals in them, and each time they're used on girls, they disrupt the vaginal mucosa. They're irritating and they will cause redness. Instead, use toilet paper, but explain that just a few sheets are necessary and not the entire roll.

Of course, you should teach your toddler to wash her hands after each time she uses the potty. Avoid relying on any hand sanitizers because some of the most common viruses that cause gastrointestinal upset don't die with hand sanitizer, so you want your toddler to clean up with soap and water in case there's any residue on their hands.

Watch for Infections

Due to the fact that many girls don't wipe correctly in the beginning, UTIs, or urinary tract infections, are more prevalent amongst potty training aged girls. When children wipe from back to front rather than front to back, they bring bacteria from their anus to their urethra. Look for signs of infection, such as frequent urination, burning or pain during urination, bloody, cloudy or foul-smelling urine, poor appetite, fever, frequent accidents, and pressure in the lower abdomen. If you notice anything like this, call your family doctor right away and they will identify it properly and recommend antibiotics as a treatment.

Offer Inspiration and Help

There are plenty of child-friendly books that are geared toward boys and girls going through potty training. There are dolls designed to help with the potty training process, such as dolls that come with little toilets that make a flushing noise and show a 'surprise' after the doll has gone potty.

Other potty training tools, such as mobile apps, can also help. These come with interactive reward charts, games and songs, and tracking tools to help both you and your little one get through the potty training process.

Chapter Seven – 12 Common Problems

In this chapter, we're going to explore twelve common concerns parents have when they're going through the potty training process, and how to handle it.

1. **Your toddler doesn't know when they need to urinate, but they recognize when they need to move their bowels.** This is completely normal. Some toddlers do not gain complete control over their bladders for months after they've learned to control their bowel movements. Keep going with potty training with this thought in mind.

2. **Your toddler tries to play with their feces.** This is just the normal curiosity of a toddler. You can prevent them from doing this without them being embarrassed or upset by telling them it's not something they should play with. Don't make a fuss about it.

3. **Your son insists he has to sit down to urinate.** The majority of boys like to sit while they learn to go in the potty. Let them learn to urinate sitting down, and after bladder control has been mastered, clarify to him that boys potty while they're standing up. Sometimes, letting him watch another man do it will prompt him to want to try.

4. **Your toddler resists being potty trained.** Resistance normally means it's not time to begin potty training yet. When your toddler seems to need a bowel movement or urinate, take them to the potty. Keep your toddler seated there for only a few minutes at a time. Explain what you're waiting for to happen, but be casual. If your toddler protests strongly, then don't insist.

5. **Your toddler is having accidents.** Accidents are going to happen. It's not called potty training for no reason. When your toddler has an accident, treat the accident lightly and don't get upset. Punishment and yelling will make children feel bad and it can make potty training take even longer.

6. **Your toddler gets upset when they see their stool being flushed away.** Some toddlers view their own excrement as being part of themselves, so it can be frightening for them to see it being flushed. Explain the purpose of bodily waste and the body's need to get rid of it.

7. **Your toddler's afraid of being sucked into the toilet.** This is a common concern for toddlers when they're first being potty trained. They're afraid they're going to get flushed down the toilet just like the rest of the stuff. To give them a feeling of control, give them pieces of toilet paper to flush so they can see what happens when they flush.

8. **Your toddler has a bowel movement or urinates as soon as they're taken off the toilet.** This occurs frequently during the early stages of potty training. It can take some time for your toddler to understand to relax the muscles that control their bladder and bowels. If this is a frequent occurrence, then your child might not be ready for potty training yet.

9. **Your toddler requests a diaper when a bowel movement is going to happen and they stand in a special area to defecate.** This is a sign that your toddler is physically, but not emotionally, ready to go through potty training. Rather than considering this a failure, praise your toddler for understanding their bowel signals. Suggest they have their bowel movement in the bathroom while they are wearing a diaper.

10. **Your toddler is having nighttime accidents.** Toddlers take longer to be completely nap-time and nighttime potty trained. Encourage them to use the bathroom before they go to bed and as soon as they wake up. Tell them that if they wake up during the middle of the night and they need to use the bathroom, they can go by themselves or ask you for help.

11. **Your toddler is only comfortable going to the bathroom with one person in particular.** This is quite normal. If your toddler will only go potty with you, then gradually withdraw from the process over time. For example, offer to help them get undressed or walk them to the bathroom, but then wait outside the door.

12. **Your toddler is regressing back to the diaper days.** Anything causing your toddler stress can encourage them to return to their previous levels of development, especially if a change has recently happened. Stressors can include illness in relatives or

themselves, babies in the house, changing from a crib to a bed, or moving to a new home. Give it time, and you'll see it pass soon. If not, refer to chapter four for more information.

Chapter Eight – Nighttime Potty Training

One of the best moments in a parent's day is when their toddler goes to sleep. Staring at that angelic face gives you the utmost joy, especially because your home is filled with the sweet sound of silence. It's even better when they're potty trained and they can wake up dry after a good night's rest. In this chapter, we're going to explore how to begin nighttime potty training, which is a bit different from daytime potty training, and might not happen until as late as six years old.

Decide if They're Ready

As your child progresses through the developmental stages, daytime potty accidents become less and less frequent, and your child starts to give you cues that they're ready to begin potty training at nighttime. If your child is starting to wake up dry from time to time, you might be ready to take the next steps. This is an exciting time for both you and your toddler, but it can be a trying time, too.

Nighttime potty training is very different from daytime potty training. The need for communication between you and your little one is extremely important. If your child cannot understand what you mean when you say the words *dry in the morning,* then they're not ready to begin nighttime potty training.

Most children will be daytime potty trained much earlier than they are nighttime potty trained. Once your child is developmentally ready, motivational strategies such as rewards can be helpful for daytime potty training, but punishments or rewards are not helpful for nighttime potty training. This is because young children do not have control over their bodily functions while they're sleeping, and they won't be woken up by their need to urinate at nighttime.

Train Their Body

If you believe it's time for you and your child to take on this challenge, then the first step is to make sure your child is kept well hydrated during the day. Don't give them anything to drink after they eat dinner, or before they head off to bed. In addition, make sure they use the potty right before they get into bed. Take a few minutes to read, or keep them occupied in some other way while they sit on the potty, giving them plenty of time to go.

Right before you go to bed around ten or eleven, gently wake your child up into a semi-awake state and take them back to the potty to urinate. The room should be dimly lit. It's important to let them know you'll be doing this, so you don't frighten or confuse them when it happens. If they resist, don't force or argue with them. Instead, let them know that they might not wish to use the potty right then, but their body might want them to use the potty. Let them keep control, but give them a way to follow through with the request. Remember to be patient at all times.

Don't force your child, but use gentle words they understand. Make sure your babysitter or nanny follows the same procedure if they're going to care for your child overnight.

You need to make sure an adult, either you or a caregiver, will be available to take your child to the potty around six or seven the next morning. Many children can make it through the night, but they need to urinate earlier in the morning before the household is fully awake.

Remain Calm

That might be easier said than done, but stress has a negative effect on a child's progress, so it's imperative you stay calm. Many parents are upset with their children that are having nighttime mishaps, but keep in mind they are not willful acts but real accidents. During the day, a child will slowly become aware of what their bladder is telling them, but at night, they have little to no control over their bodily functions.

Pull-ups and bedwetting alarms are good tools to support a child's developing nighttime training awareness. Don't push the training pace faster than your child is capable of going. Remember, a stressful situation in a child's life can cause regression and more accidents.

Remember, Accidents Happen

All children continue to wet the bed from time to time, sometimes for more than year after you think they were nighttime potty trained. This is because they are still mastering control over their bladders and their bodies. Remember, they are generally more upset by this than you are. While it's important you lavish them with praise when they succeed, it's just as important to comfort them when they don't. Do not use embarrassment as a training method, or react as if there was a big problem. This is important for your child, and your child's siblings, to see and mirror.

If your child's accidents are consistent, then you might want to talk to the family doctor to make sure there isn't an underlying medical issue. Keep in mind that girls tend to be trained quicker than boys. Many girls are fully nighttime trained around six, but most boys are not fully nighttime trained until they're around seven.

Appreciate This Stage

As your child grows older, their motivation to wake up dry each morning is going to grow. Continually washing wet sheets is not exactly fun, but remember, this is one of the many developmental milestones that mark your child's growth, mastery of life, and independence. As frustrating as it seems, try to enjoy this bit of time you have with your child.

It'll go by quickly!

Chapter Nine – Constipation

Constipation in children is a serious condition that can cause potty training issues, and can even cause physical issues later on in life. That's why it's imperative to begin looking for constipation as soon as your child is born, but even more so during potty training exercises.

To tell if your child is constipated, look for the following signs:

- In newborns, firm stool that occurs less than once per day, but with difficulty and straining, is constipation.
- Hard, dry stool and pain when passing it is constipation.
- A pebble-like, hard stool passed by babies who strain during bowel movements, grunt, draw their legs up to the abdomen, and get red-faced is constipation.
- Streaks of blood on the exterior of the stool is constipation.
- Abdominal distress, along with hard, irregular stool, is another sign of constipation.

Causes

As the digested food travels through the intestines, nutrients and water are absorbed, and the waste turns into a stool. For a soft stool to be made, enough water has to stay in the waste material, and the lower rectal and intestinal muscles have to relax and contract to move the stool along and out of the body. Malfunction of either of these mechanisms, such as not enough water or poor muscle movements, causes constipation.

Being plugged up with hard stool for three days can be uncomfortable.

Constipation can turn into a self-perpetuating issue. Hard stool will cause pain when it passes; therefore, the child holds onto the stool. The longer the stool is inside, the harder it will become, which will make it even more painful to pass the stool. The muscle tone becomes weaker the longer the stool is in there to stretch the intestinal wall. To complicate everything, passage of hard stool through a narrow rectum can cause a tear in the rectal wall, which is known as a rectal fissure. This creates the streaks of blood. This painful tear will make babies not want to have bowel movements even more.

Causes of constipation in infants include:

- New milks or foods. If your baby has begun a new food, switched from formula to breast milk or vice versa, or to cow's formula, they could be experiencing constipation due to this abrupt change in diet. Return to a looser-stool diet they're used to and slowly switch over. If you can't, then contact a pediatrician about the proper procedure for switching.
- For an infant fed using bottles, consider experimenting with different formulas to figure out the one that's best for them. In addition, give a formula-fed baby an extra bottle of water daily.

Causes of constipation in children include:

- Toddlers going through negative phases or emotional upsets can have a reluctance having a bowel movement. When people are upset, sometimes their intestines can be affected. This can cause diarrhea, too.
- Your toddler might not be drinking enough fluids during the day. Consider giving them two to three extra glasses of water or some diluted juice.
- They might not be getting enough fiber in their diet. Consider serving more fresh fruits and vegetables at snack time.

Treatment

Try this ten step plan to treat constipation in toddlers.

1. **Serve more fluids.** Not drinking enough fluids is a subtle contributor to issues when it comes to constipation, especially for young children. The colon is the body regulator of fluids. If a person is not getting enough fluids, their colon steals water from their waste material and gives it to their body, causing their stool to be water-deprived and hard. People who have diets high in fiber need to increase their water consumption along with their fiber-rich foods because fiber must have water to do the intestinal cleanup job. More fluids in a child's diet will put more fluids in their bowels, which will lessen constipation.

2. **Add more fiber-rich foods to their diets.** Fiber will soften the stool by drawing more water to them, making them easier to pass because they're bulkier. Fiber foods for toddlers include graham crackers, bran cereals, whole grain crackers and breads, and high fiber vegetables such as broccoli, peas, and beans.

3. **Get them more exercise.** Exercise will improve digestion and speed the passage of food through the intestines, which means less of a chance for it to sit and have more water sucked from it.

4. **Ease the passage.** Infants might need some help from their parents with some well-timed suppositories. As they go through the phase of learning how to have bowel movements, many babies in the early months will draw up their knees and grunt to push out their stool. However, the straining baby might appreciate some outside help with a glycerin suppository. These are available without prescription at pharmacies and look like little rocket ships. If the baby is straining, insert one as far into the rectum as you can and hold their behind together for a few minutes to dissolve the glycerin. These are helpful for lubricating the baby's rectum if there is a tear or bleeding. Don't use for more than a few days without a doctor's permission.

5. **Wiggle it out.** As soon as the glycerin suppository is in, wiggle it a little, which will stimulate the tense muscles to relax and ease the passage of the stool.

6. **Insert the liquid glycerin.** This is also known as Babylax, which can be inserted into the baby's rectum with a dropper and will stimulate a bowel movement.

7. **Use a natural laxative.** When you're using a laxative, try the most natural one first. Start with diluted prune juice with the pulp. Two- to six-month-old infants should have a tablespoon or two and toddlers should have up to eight ounces. Try strained prunes or make a puree yourself by stewing your own. You can serve it straight or disguised, or spread it on some crackers. Apricots, plums, pears, and peaches are all laxatives, too. If these are not sufficient, then try:

   a. **Psyllium Husks.** These are available at nutrition stores, and are natural fiber stool softeners. This is a bland laxative that can be served over cereal or combined with a fruit and yogurt puree. Toddlers should start with one teaspoon per day and increase to two as needed. Be sure to serve it with eight ounces of water. For this fiber to work, the intestines require a lot of fluid; otherwise, the psyllium gums up and can cause worse issues.

8. **Nonprescription laxatives.** Malt-barley extracts and psyllium powders can soften your child's stool, as well as these other options:

   a. **Flax Oil.** This is a favorite for most children. It's a healthy alternative to mineral oil, which is not only a laxative, but gives your child a good dose of omega-3 fats, too. While you might hear that mineral oil is good to relieve constipation, due to it being a mixture of hydrocarbons made from petroleum products, most people are not convinced of its safety. In addition, unlike mineral oil, flax oil is a nutrient that helps the absorption of

> vitamins. Infants can have up to a teaspoon a day, toddlers two, and children one tablespoon.
>
> b. **Flax Seed Meal.** This is ground flax seed, and it's a better laxative than the oil because it has fiber in it. It looks similar to finely ground bran flakes and mixes well with soupy cereals, or can be added to high-fiber smoothies. The dosage of this is one tablespoon per day for toddlers and two tablespoons for older children.

9. **Suppositories.** Besides the glycerin suppositories alone, try suppositories that also contain a laxative ingredient. These can be used from time to time if the constipation is resistant to the simpler measures.

10. **Use enemas as last resorts.** Babies who are constipated chronically can try something like Baby Fleet, which is an enema available without prescription, and directions are on the package.

The above methods are general tips for treating or preventing constipation for all ages, but these are tips specific to infants. It's important to keep the bowels moving healthily at an early stage because it prevents issues down the road.

1. If you're using formula, experiment with different ones to figure out which is most friendly to your baby's intestines.

2. Feed your infant smaller amounts of formula at more frequent intervals. This gives the intestines a good chance of properly digesting the formula. One way to do this is feed half as much twice as often.

3. Delay introducing solid foods for those who are constipated, such as bananas and rice. Rather than rice cereal, try some barley cereal. Good starter foods for infants that are high in fiber are pureed prunes and pears.

4. Used the glycerin suppositories to ease the passage of stools as described above.

5. Add a teaspoon of flax oil into your baby's cereal or their bottle.

6. Watch out for signs they're about to go. As soon as they start to grimace, grunt, strain, or look bloated, quickly insert the suppository.

Bath and Bowel Movement Technique

A trick that many parents will use to help ease the passage of their infant or toddler's stools is to use the bath technique. It's messy, but it works. Immerse your baby in the warm bath water so it's surrounding them chest-high. When they're relaxed in the bathtub, massage their belly and they'll have a bowel movement.

Iron-Fortified Formula and Constipation

Before you rush into attributing the constipation of your baby to the iron in the formula, you might be interested in knowing that controlled studies performed by Dr. Oski, the Professor and Chairman of the Department of Pediatrics at John Hopkins, demonstrated that iron-fortified formulas didn't cause constipation any more than a formula that didn't have iron.

However, scientific research and mother's observations tend to clash. Pediatricians will continue to tell you to feed your child an iron-fortified formula for a reason. Low-iron formulas will not provide your baby with enough amounts of iron, which will result in anemia between the ages of six months to one year.

If you're certain the iron-fortified formula is contributing to constipation, use the treatments recommended to treat constipation. If your child is still constipated, then try the low-iron formula for two months only. Then, once their intestines are more mature and their tolerance has increased, switch back to the fortified formula.

Toddler's Holding onto Bowel Movements

Constipation is one of the most perplexing and uncomfortable problems in young children. This is how the system is normally supposed to work. The presence of a lot of stool in the large intestine will signal the urge to go to the bathroom. The child will respond to this signal or choose to ignore it if they are too busy doing something else.

Unlike the urge to urinate, which children cannot control for too long, they can choose to ignore their signal to go number two. The longer your child ignores it, the more the fluid in the restrained stool will be absorbed and the harder the stool will become. It will then hurt to go to the bathroom, which will cause your child to hold it even longer, and the vicious cycle will start. Your child will hold onto their stool for longer and longer and become more and more constipated.

Try the following steps with a toddler who is going through this cycle.

1. Make a diagram of their large intestine or print one out from online, showing the large golf balls of stool at the end of their large intestine. Show them that voluntarily holding this in will make them harder, and that is why it's hurting them when the stool passes.
2. Encourage them to have bowel movements at specific times during the day, especially after they eat breakfast.
3. Encourage them to respond to their urge to go immediately, and convey to them that they should go when they have to go.

If your child has had this issue for a long time, the intestinal muscles can become weak. It might be necessary to try stool softeners for up to a month to correct the issue.

Potty Training in 3 Days

Potty training your toddler can happen in three days, but don't get frustrated if it doesn't work the first time. There are some rare toddlers who just aren't ready yet. However, if you believe your child is ready for potty training, by all means try this three-day method.

Some things to do with this training method are:

1. Keep them naked from the waist down.
2. Keep them in a restricted area close to the bathroom.

Day One: Learning What the Potty Is

On the first day, wake up your toddler, or wait until they decide to get up, then take them to the bathroom as soon as they get up. If you happen to catch them before they use their diaper, you can start off on the right foot and have them use the potty right away. However, don't be disappointed or upset if you don't get to them soon enough. You can move on to the following step.

The second step is to wait twenty minutes. You're going to take your toddler to the bathroom quite often throughout the day. It should be every twenty minutes, which is three times an hour. Take them to the bathroom, put them on their training potty, and tell them in a happy voice to go to the bathroom. Make sure you're positive! This shouldn't ever be a negative experience for your toddler.

They won't be able to pee every twenty minutes. You're just teaching them to sit on the potty and try to go. They'll be able to go every couple of times, hopefully, or about every hour or two hours.

This might not occur on the first day. The idea is to get them to push and try every time they sit on the potty. They should have gone once or twice by the end of your first day. Even a little bit of pee when they sit down is amazing progress! You're helping them avoid an accident by giving them many chances to use the bathroom.

You don't have to praise them insanely every time they sit on the potty. If they try but don't happen to produce anything, tell them, "Good try." Every time they sit down is helpful in terms of teaching them how to use the bathroom. Save your excited praise for the actual event. You want them to be excited when you're excited because this gives them the motivation to keep trying to use the bathroom.

When they begin peeing on the floor (and they will), run over to them as soon as you see it happen. Pick them up and take them to the potty to use it. When you see them beginning to pee on the floor, tell them, "Pee-pee doesn't go on the floor, it goes in the potty!" Do this every time. This is the reason you should restrict their space and keep them naked.

Being on the other side of the house, away from the potty, when this happens will be difficult to handle. On the other hand, being only a few steps away from the bathroom will make this process a lot easier, as they'll still be peeing when you get them to the potty. Praise them if they end up getting a few dribbles in the potty. This will reinforce the idea of peeing in the potty.

For example, if you catch your toddler beginning to pee on the floor, pick them up quickly and tell them that pee goes in the potty. Take them a few steps to the potty and sit them down so they can finish in the training potty. When they finish, that's a success! Cheer and smile; show your toddler the pee in the training potty. Then have them help you carry that to the potty and flush it. Showing them the flushing of their urine reinforces the idea that this is normal.

It's important to have your toddler wash their hands with you and to tell them you're proud of them for going to the bathroom on the potty. Then go back to the designated area and show them where they went on the floor. Tell them that they don't pee on the floor, it's gross, and that pee goes in the potty. Point to the potty, then clean up the mess. Repeat this for three days. If they don't go again within twenty minutes, take them to the potty and have them try to go. Repeat this every twenty minutes.

Now that you have demonstrated to them what will happen, you must keep it up! That means every twenty minutes for the entire day for three days. They should be naked all throughout the day, except for naptime and bedtime. Nighttime potty training is different from daytime potty training.

Consider it a success if your toddler attempts to go to the potty, pees on the potty, or acknowledges that they have had an accident when they have pee running down their legs. This is going to be the case for most kids, starting around the middle of the first day. Every child will be different; their personalities are different, so the rate at which they learn to go on the potty will be different. Some will be trained within a day or two, while others will need a few more days to practice.

Day Two: Accident-Free Time

On the first day, your toddler doesn't really get the idea, but they'll learn that they need to go to the bathroom on the potty and not on the floor. On the second day, you'll be expanding on that idea, helping them grasp it. By the second day, most kids will almost completely stop having accidents and will use the potty about seventy percent of the time.

If your toddler is using the potty more than half the time, it's safe to take them from going to the potty every twenty minutes to going to the potty every half an hour to forty minutes. If you feel that they'd benefit from a second day of every-twenty-minutes, by all means go for it. It'll only help your toddler, not hinder them. Two days of every-twenty-minutes should be enough to get the idea to sink into your child's mind; however, if they aren't making it after two days, you might want to think about holding off for a few more weeks and trying again in the future.

If you really feel up to it, you can try the every-twenty-minutes method for a third day. You're using the same idea as on day one, but you're increasing the amount of time between trips. You still need to stay in the potty training area, especially if they're having a lot of accidents. If they're using the potty on demand or not experiencing accidents, this might work. They'll still have some accidents, so keep that in mind when you decide to expand their area.

Remember, keep your toddler in a diaper at night and during naptime. Sleep potty training will take some time, and while it can be done, you're already going to be exhausted from trying to complete daytime potty training in three days. Don't overwhelm yourself or your toddler. If you're feeling up to it, you can try it now, but never get upset or angry if your child continues to have nighttime accidents. Some toddlers aren't nighttime trained until they're well above the age of two.

Day Three: Increase the Time

On the third day, you can try to have your toddler go every hour rather than every half an hour. They should still be naked in the morning. You'll still want to keep them in their confined area, such as on a single floor of your home if you have two stories, or close to some bedroom doors if you're in a single-story home or apartment. Keep them close, but you don't have to stay in the close quarters you were in before. Keep taking your toddler to the potty every hour, or more often if you have to. Your toddler should be using the potty and not having many accidents now if you're able to catch them on time.

You're going to miss a few accidents, but that's alright. Halfway through this day, when you feel pretty confident that your toddler is getting the idea, you can move them into underwear. This is going to be difficult for them to understand and it's when you're going to want to give up because it feels like a diaper for them.

It's a little confusing for them, so you need to stay on top of them to look for signs that they need to go. Pee running down their legs or pee in their underwear are both signs that you should get them to the potty quickly. Also do this if they start to take off their underwear. Your toddler is going to have a few accidents on this day. They'll begin peeing in their underwear. They might look sad about this or they might not care at all, but you should stick with it. Don't give up!

Some toddlers really struggle with the concept of underwear. When you put the underwear on them, they immediately begin peeing in it. Your toddler might feel like the underwear is a diaper. Sometimes, you might have to leave them in their clean underwear and take them to the potty every twenty minutes to help them get used to the feel. Do this for the entire third day.

You can extend the potty training another day or two. When the third day comes to a close, remember that you'll be in the training stage for about a month. However, your toddler should understand the basic concept of going potty on the toilet and not in their underwear or diaper. They probably won't have an accident if you're on top of it, such as by taking them to the potty every hour or so. You'll know how often your toddler has to go, so be sure to take them during those times.

For the first few weeks, you'll want to keep your toddler naked from the waist down as much as possible until you feel confident that they won't be having any additional accidents. If you're home, keep them naked or in their underwear at all times, for around a month. It's still going to be weeks or months before your toddler lets you know they have to go without being reminded. They may not have accidents during this time, but they could hold their pee until you take them to go.

Take them every hour or so for a few hours, regardless of whether they show signs of needing to go. This will eliminate accidents. If you need to go out, remember that your child should go to the bathroom before you leave, and then again when you arrive wherever you're going. You might want to take them a little more often to avoid accidents outside the home during those first few months.

Don't leave home without your travel potty. If you don't want to take your toddler to the potty where you're going, have them go with the travel potty before you get out of the car.

Here's a huge reminder for all parents who are potty training their toddler in three days – it's difficult for your toddler to tell you when they have to go because they don't recognize the sensation yet, so you need to watch for signs from them that they need to use the potty. These signs could be holding themselves, trying to hide, or dancing around. Remember, they'll most likely learn when they need to pee by having a few accidents on the floor or in their underwear, and then they'll realize that urine is coming out.

Once they've seen you and experienced your taking them to the potty, they'll learn that they should be on the potty when this happens. This is alright; it's how they learn. They might start to acknowledge that they need to go by repeating a phrase you say, such as "uh-oh" or "oh-no".

Just remember, stick to the plan.

Toddlers aren't born knowing how to use the bathroom, so you have to train them. Just as you train your toddler to drink from a cup, write their name, or tie their shoes, you need to train them to use the toilet.

Regression

So many parents try this method and then complain about regression after their toddler was seemingly trained. Regression is normal after a big event, such as a move or the birth of another child. No matter what the case may be, regression is a common occurrence. Try not to potty train your toddler around a big event, such as moving or a sibling's birth. Train them a month or two before another child is born.

It might be wise to train them after the new addition to the family has been born, but you also might be too exhausted to do so. Having accidents after being potty trained is totally normal. The toddler starts to see what it's like to be a baby again and to not have the responsibility of using the potty, so they start trying to need diapers again. Be prepared with a plan.

You can go back to the weekend-being-naked plan, but it can be a little more laidback. Try starting at the day-two method again. Correct them when they have an accident, and plan on spending a few days getting them back on track. They'll come around eventually. Just stick to the plan.

Punishment for children who regress isn't usually the answer; however, a few children regress simply for attention. You'll know when your child is doing this. They won't care that they've regressed and that they're having accidents. This is when it's time to use some timeouts to teach them that their behavior isn't appropriate. For a two-year-old, a simple timeout of two minutes will suffice.

However, timeouts should be used only if there is a discipline problem with your child, not simply because they had an accident. You don't want to punish them for something they're unable to control yet. Be consistent with children who have regressed. This is the most important aspect of potty training for any toddler.

Don't go back to diapers if you can help it. Remember, use positive reinforcement. Cheer and dance when they have a success! If you can make the experience positive and reward them with good attention for going to the bathroom, they'll want to go to the bathroom.

They Won't Poop on the Potty

What if your toddler will pee on the potty, but won't go number two? Once you've trained your toddler in three days, you might run into this hurdle. This is the biggest concern for most parents trying this method.

For example, one parent had to deal with a child who would come home from school, put on a diaper, and poop in the diaper. He was seven! Many parents are terrified that this will be their child. Once your child gets over the fear of going on the potty, they'll use the potty consistently for everything.

So why won't your toddler poop on the potty? They're afraid. They literally believe their poop is a part of them, and a part of them is falling off. It sounds ridiculous, but every doctor out there has given the same answer. Some people like to use anatomy books to show their children that food goes in and comes out. One idea is to feed them corn so they see it in the potty when they go. It's gross, but it makes sense. The corn shows them that their poop isn't part of their body, and it really is food.

Another reason they might be resisting going number two on the potty is that their bowel movements could be painful. They might be holding it too long, and then when they decide to go, it hurts. Your child might remember one painful experience for quite some time. This lessens their urge to want to try again.

Talk to your pediatrician about easy solutions, such as foods, oils, and drinks that will make going to the bathroom easier. You don't want your toddler to become constipated, ever! Some doctors recommend Miralax for children who are constipated.

It could take a few months before your toddler decides that they can go poop on the potty. Some children will go pee and poop on the potty within three days. It just depends on the toddler.

How can you get them to go poop on the potty, too? Here are a few tips.

1. Try putting your toddler on the potty over a towel in front of the television. Put on their favorite show and wait. Your toddler will just sit there, naked, watching their show until they're ready to go poop. If they're not ready and they get up, turn off the show and do something else for a bit. Keep repeating this until they poop on the potty.

2. Let them have a treat while they're waiting on the potty. Some people like to use ice cream, while others like to use their child's favorite snack. Just make sure it's something they really enjoy. You don't want to do this with everything, but using food for a few days while you try to get them to go poop on the potty will pay off in the long run.

3. Try both methods. Sit your toddler on the potty in front of the television and give them a lollipop or some ice cream. If they get up without going, take away the treat. Your toddler might cry the first few times you do this until they realize they're allowed to have the treat if they sit on the potty. Don't force your toddler to sit on the potty. The idea of a reward will keep them on the potty.

If you're keeping the potty in the bathroom, try talking to your toddler. Tell them a story or keep them talking about a story about what they did during the day. By distracting them with a story, music, or a game, you'll keep them from being afraid of going poop, and they'll feel relaxed enough to go. While they're on the potty, try playing a movie or a song for them from your phone.

Really reward your child for this. Buy some special coloring books, prizes, or treats. These rewards are only if you have issues with one major part of potty training and when a little extra help will go a long way toward getting them to do what you'd like them to do. In most cases, your toddler should get a reward only when they go poop on the potty. Once they do this the first time, it'll be much easier in the future. Occasionally, they'll regress in terms of going number two. Don't give up. Go back to them being naked for a few days and keep repeating the process.

At some point in time, your toddler might have a stomach illness and you'll want to go back to the diapers for this. If they have diarrhea, this changes things. Don't tell your toddler they're wearing a diaper. Tell them you're putting them in special underwear while they're sick. If they've been potty trained for a few months, you most likely won't need to do this. They'll understand when they need to go to the potty.

Give it some time and keep trying. You want to try first thing in the morning. If you're worried they're completely avoiding going number two in order to go potty on the toilet, let them have a diaper at naptime and bedtime. They'll go in their diaper. Don't let your toddler get constipated over the fear of having an accident, so if they poop while they're sleeping during naptime, let it happen for now. Keep trying when they get up, too.

Handling Accidents

How do you handle it when your toddler poops in their pants? Just keep telling your toddler "no" when they poop in their pants. It's disgusting, so let them know you don't approve of what they did. To clean it up, take the dirty underwear and put the poop in the potty while your toddler watches, and then flush it.

Next, take the soiled underwear to the washer and keep your toddler watching. The entire time, act as if this is gross and that you don't approve. You don't need to be mean, but be upset.

Remember, this will pass, like everything else. If you suspect your child has a medical condition that is interfering with their ability to go to the potty, you should resolve it before you potty train.

Potty Training a Toddler with Special Needs

Potty training children with special needs is a little more challenging, but it's possible. The average age for potty training a child with special needs – around four or five years – is higher than the average age for potty training other children. Don't feel defeated if your neighbor's toddler is potty trained and you're still working on potty training your four-year-old. Every child is unique, and you must do what works for them.

While no parent wants to push their child with special needs to do what they can't do, if you can help them use the toilet, the change in their self-esteem will be amazing. It's such an accomplishment for them, and they feel proud, as should you.

Before you begin training, have a quick talk with a doctor and therapist about any concerns you might have. They'll give you advice that's specific to your child. This is imperative, so don't skip this step. Have a physical done before you move forward with potty training; make sure your toddler doesn't have any infections or constipation issues.

First, watch for the signs that they need to go. You need to see the same ones that someone would see in a toddler. Are they staying dry for an hour or more? Are they showing signs before they have a bowel movement? Do they seem interested in the bathroom or in you when you use the potty?

If your child is hesitant or resisting, you need to wait. This is very true for a special needs situation. Don't worry about it now. Just pick it back up when your child seems interested.

If you believe your child is ready to learn, prepare them for what's about to happen. They'll begin using the bathroom, flushing the toilet loudly, and washing their hands with warm water. They'll wear underwear with some of their favorite things on it.

Things you might want to remember before you jump in:

1. It's alright that they're older. This is their time.
2. The process can take longer; a weekend isn't going to work. That's alright.
3. You'll need to do a little more with them, such as help with their clothing and the toilet, and wash their hands.
4. Accidents are going to happen. Be prepared, both physically and emotionally.
5. Your family must be prepared. You might need a break or someone to help or even just someone who can listen. Tell them what you're doing. Their support is extremely important for you and your child.
6. Do this with your child as a team. Look at everything you and your child have done together so far.
7. Every child is different, and the advice you find in this book may or may not help your child. That's fine because you'll learn what works for them.

Different Types of Delays

Physical

These can make the process of training your child more difficult. Try offering a stool for your child's feet, or install a bar next to the toilet to help them gain their balance. Remember, plan for what you'll need when your child is using the toilet. Are you going to help them? Are they going to need your assistance permanently? Will they be able to do this on their own if they have special areas, such as the support bars, prepared for them?

Visual

Visual disabilities make it hard for children when they're starting to potty train. They're not able to observe someone else using the bathroom. They're not able to see you walk to the toilet, to see how you reach to flush the potty and how you turn on the water to check for the temperature when you wash your hands. You have to tell them these things.

They'll rely more on their other senses, such as sound, smell, and touch. Children with visual delays might have a harder time being potty trained at first. It's important to leave the training toilet in a single spot; don't move it. Through touch, you'll need to show your child how to use only a certain amount of toilet paper, how to sit on the potty every time, and what to do afterwards. Teach them how to find the sink and soap.

Here are a few tips:

1. Keep the bathroom smelling nice and clean. Smell is a huge factor for children with visual problems.
2. Let them explore the bathroom after it's been cleaned to make the experience pleasant, and encourage your child to be in there.
3. Let your child put their hand on yours so they can find what you're referring to by exploring it with you.

Hearing

Kids who are hearing imparied might have a hard time if you're still having difficulties communicating with them. They can't call out to tell you they need help. Remember to pay close attention and communicate with them. Adapt your method of communication to fit your child's needs.

Here are a few tips to help:

1. Let them watch you use the bathroom.
2. Look through books about toilet training and learn the appropriate sign language with them.
3. Use the same sign every time.

Remember, being audibly verbal doesn't have to stop you.

Cerebral Palsy

Children who have cerebral palsy have a harder time with toilet training because their ability to determine when they have to go develops much later than it does in other children. For example, a three-year-old with cerebral palsy might become fidgety when they have to go, but that's the only sign you have before they lose their bowels or bladder.

Children with this condition might have a hard time staying on the potty. Make sure to use a special chair with a high back and bars on the sides so they're able to keep themselves on the potty. Some parents like to sit on the toilet with their child in front of them to give them more support.

Behavioral Disorders

Many parents who have children with autism or a sensory disorder are concerned about potty training their children. It doesn't have to be a daunting, frightening task for either you or your child!

Potty training a child with behavioral issues is a challenge because you know that while they can physically do it, the disorder is stopping them. Still, it's possible. You'll really need to know them and what motivates them to do their best.

Children like this are often motivated by praise from their parent. You could offer a small reward, such as a sticker, for doing a good job and attempting to use the bathroom without getting frustrated. Normally, parents shouldn't use charts or rewards like this, but this situation is unique.

Remember, you're changing their routine, so they're going to need to adjust to the new one – taking off their clothes, using the bathroom where they haven't spent any time, and learning how to wash their hands. Still, almost all children with behavioral issues can be potty trained.

Here are a few tips to remember:

1. Before you begin, have your child examined by a professional to rule out any medical conditions, such as UTI's or constipation.
2. Observe your child's patterns to see if something in particular is troubling them about this process. Maybe the floor's too cold and some slippers by the bathroom door are in order, or maybe the smell is off-putting and you need to find a cleaner that smells better to them.
3. Observe the times they have to go. How long after they eat or drink do they normally have to urinate or defecate? Do certain drinks or foods give them problems?
4. Explain everything to them, and then explain it again. Use charts to demonstrate to them what's happening.
5. If your child doesn't want to go to the potty, try using a reward.
6. Don't get angry with them. Instead, try to be consistent. You just want to keep taking them to the potty, and they'll learn that they go a few time a day, so it's a routine.

Remember, the entire process is a learning curve for both of you. Have patience, don't yell, and don't ever make your child feel as though they're not good enough because they're not learning quick enough. They'll learn at their own pace, and you'll be all that much more grateful when they do!

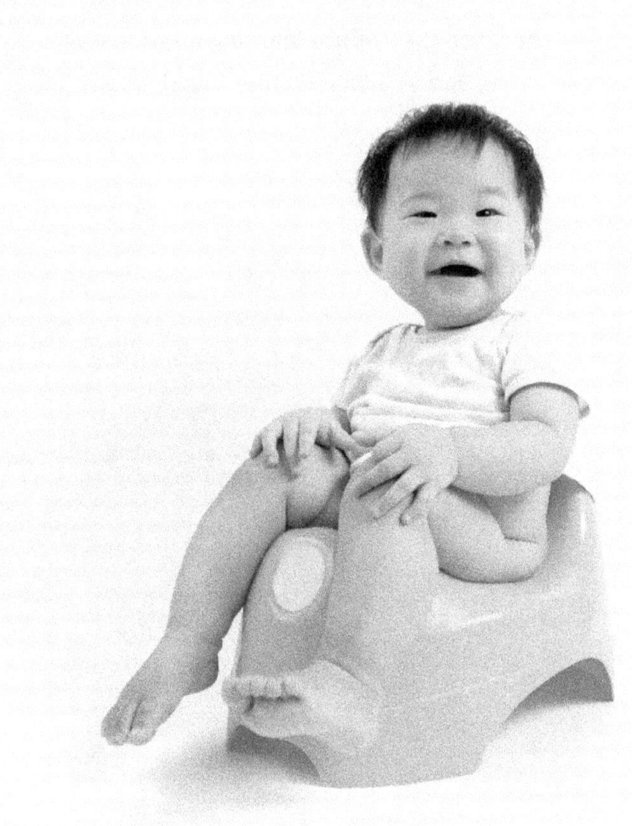

Conclusion

Most parents believe that if their baby is not potty trained by the age of three, there is something wrong with their potty training technique or with the child. If the concern is over nighttime bedwetting and bowel movements, then don't sweat it. A majority of children will not be able to make it through the night without wetting the bed until they're around five or six years old. They will have the occasional accident, and getting upset about it is not going to help the situation.

Many authority figures who are not properly educated about children's bathroom habits and developmental stages believe all children should be completely potty trained by the time they're three or four – namely, preschool staff. It is imperative to not allow those who have not been trained in the medical industry to determine when it's time to potty train your child.

You are your toddler's parent, and you and your child should be the ones who determine when it's right for your toddler to be potty trained. Trust your instincts, and if you have any concerns about constipation or other potential medical issues, speak with a certified pediatrician.

I hope you found useful information in this book. If you did, please leave a review at your online eBook retailer's website. Each review will help other parents like you find useful information to help them through the potty training process.

Thank you for reading!

BONUS: Daily Routine for Toddlers

Routine is imperative for a child, no matter what their age is. While some of the items listed in this routine may seem trivial to a parent, they are not trivial for your toddler. They teach your toddler important life skills, so don't skimp on things like play dates and time with you!

Let's look at a few key points to a toddler's routine before you see a sample.

Sleep

No matter what schedule your toddler has, from the age of two to three, your baby needs around fourteen hours of sleep a day. Some will need a little less while others need a little more, but this is pretty consistent with all the schedules parents have shared over the years. Some toddlers will sleep more during the night and have a short nap, while others might sleep a little less at night and take a longer nap during the day.

However, fourteen hours overall is the goal you should aim for.

Naptime

Parents across the globe have come to the consensus that having your toddler wake up about four hours before they are to go to bed helps them sleep well at night. Having a toddler take a nap about an hour after they eat lunch is another great time for them. If you can find a good balance between those two time ranges, then you'll have a successful naptime.

Wakeup Time and Bedtime

One of the things sleep experts tend to recommend is wake up times being between six and eight in the morning and six and eight at night. If your toddler wakes up early, around six in the morning, then you might want to have an earlier bedtime of around six thirty to seven thirty. If your family needs a bit more evening time together, then you might like a later bedtime of eight if your toddler can sleep a bit later in the morning.

Incorporating Independent Playtime

If you're someone who's busy at home, then independent playtime is a good way to get more things done throughout the day, and it's a good way to teach your toddler some independence. While your toddler plays alone in a safe environment, you can get as much done as you can, and for the rest of the day, you're fully engaged with your baby.

Incorporating Routines

Routines are an excellent way to minimize nagging, yelling, and reminding throughout the day. Routines are simple to follow steps for your toddler that trigger them to do certain things without your say-so. Toddlers learn what's expected of them, and a routine helps them feel they have a sense of control over their daily lives.

You might think that'd be the opposite, but it's not. Toddlers feel a sense of control when they master a routine well, and they know what to expect on a daily basis, which is comforting.

Here are a few small routines to follow:

- Pre-mealtime Routine: Wash hands, help set the table, sit at the tale, etc.

- Pre-bedtime Routine: Brush teeth, take a bath, put on pajamas, read quietly, have a snack, bedtime.

Routines should be simple and shouldn't take a lot of time.

Example Toddler Schedule

- 8 am – wake up, have a diaper change (or go to the bathroom), and eat breakfast.

- 8:30 am – structured playtime with Mom or Dad, or go to preschool.

- 9:30 am – independent playtime.

- 10:30 am – eat a snack, have some free playtime inside, and outside time if the weather permits.

- 12 pm – eat lunch.

- 1 pm – take a nap.

- 3:30 pm – wake up from the nap, have a small snack, watch a little television, and then free playtime.

- 5 pm – eat dinner

- 6 pm – take a bath

- 6:30 pm – bedtime routine (brush teeth, take a bath, read, etc.)

- 7 pm – bedtime

ABOUT THE AUTHOR

Merry Palmer is a California licensed family therapist, speaker and parenting trainer in Los Angeles. She is also the author and co-author of several bestselling parenting books.

For the last 10 years Merry teaches parents and child care professionals as a popular speaker and trainer at numerous early childhood conferences, workshops and trainings.

She lives and works in Los Angeles, California.

Merry and her husband Richard have two sons and daughter.

Find my other books on AMAZON

www.amazon.com/author/merry.palmer

Copyright 2017
Published in the United States by Merry Palmer / © Merry Palmer-
All rights Reserved. No part of this publication or the information in it may be quoted from or reproduced in any form by means such as printing, scanning, photocopying or otherwise without prior written permission of the copyright holder.
Disclaimer and Terms of Use: Effort has been made to ensure that the information in this book is accurate and complete, however, the author and the publisher do not warrant the accuracy of the information, text and graphics contained within the book due to the rapidly changing nature of science, research, known and unknown facts and internet. The Author and the publisher do not hold any responsibility for errors, omissions or contrary interpretation of the subject matter herein. This book is presented solely for motivational and informational purposes only.